My Shadow

Robert Louis Stevenson

Illustrated by Glenna Lang

Columbus, OH

Illustrations by Glenna Lang from MY SHADOW by Robert Louis Stevenson. Reprinted by permission of David R. Godine, Publisher, Inc. Copyright © 1989 by Glenna Lang.

SRAonline.com

SRA

Printed in the U.S.A.

Send all inquiries to:
SRA/McGraw-Hill
4400 Easton Commons
Columbus, OH 43219-6188

ISBN 978-0-07-612277-6
MHID 0-07-612277-8

10 11 12 LHN 21

The McGraw·Hill Companies

My Shadow

For Esmé

I have a little shadow that goes in and out with me,

And what can be the use of him is more than I can see.

He is very, very like me from the heels up to the head;

And I see him jump before me,

when I jump into my bed.

The funniest thing about him

is the way he likes to grow—

Not at all like proper children,

which is always very slow;

For he sometimes shoots up taller,

like an India-rubber ball,

And he sometimes gets so little

that there's none of him at all.

He hasn't got a notion of how children ought to play,

And can only make a fool of me in every sort of way.

He stays so close beside me,

he’s a coward you can see;

I’d think shame to stick to nursie

as that shadow sticks to me!

One morning, very early,

before the sun was up,

I rose and found the shining dew on every buttercup;

But my lazy little shadow, like an arrant sleepy head,

Had stayed at home behind me and was fast asleep in bed.